Nat Shazi

Rain, Screened, Backporch

WungGong

SansEra

ASAT

Mystery of Non-Existance

Printed in the United States of America

Cover and Book design by Nat Shazi

Printed and bound by www.Lulu.com

Library of Congress Cataloging-in -Publication Data

Shazi, Nat
  Rain, Screened, Backporch: poems, short stories /
SansEra
    P.cm.
  ISBN 978-0-6152-0774-2
I. Title

                                              ID: 2134370

Lulu Enterprises, Inc.
860 Aviation Parkway,
        Suite 300
Morrisville, NC. 27560

I.

Preface
By Nat Shazi

The 'Mystery of Non-existence', Asat is found in the Dharmalaksana school. It is the mind-theory or origination from phenomenal consciousness, Mere-consciousness school. Here, in these simple poems, serious, humorous, witty and straight forward the 'Great Mystery' is pointed to.

Spending nearly 40 years meditating, writing poetry for 30 years, and painting for 25 years. Brought home here to my own den where I found the Dharmalaksana school. After having searched 20 years for the Samdhinirmocana Mayhayana Sutra. Presented in the poem '10,000 Mile Railroad Track'. Being the 'Featured Poet' twice on thegoldenlantern.com, a Buddhist, Taoist poetry page. With several of my paintings also shown.

The Continuum that remains is revealed in the paintings presented here. The style, technique in the paintings being present before I studied the art masters. Meditating my art in 'Sikan Taza', (theme less meditation) it came out. I somehow already had the art skill. 'Sijo' poems because for me they are just fun to write and I like the surprise twist at the end. Waka and Tanka in style most of the other poems. Presenting a panoramic view of an insight derived from my meditations.

The Children's stories written with a heightened awareness background. Each having a subject that can be pondered over and learned from.

Direct experiences put into poem form are the Shamanistic stories. Real 'Ywepi' men and women practicing their trade.

'Antidotal Healing Remedies, take the medicine', meant as a tribute to Allen Ginsberg for his last book, 'Death & Fame'. Any one from the list can cure your afflictions and attachments. Dharma practice: psychological and emotional well being is discovered in the experiences of study, meditations and applications which reveals the essences of highest truth.. Bhutatathata:

Real nature of Mere-Consciousness' (chen-ru). Chen means real. Ru (suchness) means always such. Parinespanna (the perfect). It is the ultimate reality.

It is the true nature of dharma; or elements of existence; suchness, (tathata) and emptiness' (sunyata);

it is without origination as it does not change.

III.

Transmigrations oppose 'Nirvana'. The Bhutatathata or absolute in Tran migratory forms.

The absolute perfect reality is here and now. This knowing is the same now as it will always be. There is no nirvana to be obtained. Just this Transmigration flowing and returning, flowing back again within samsara.

That-that-I-am is real and always such. There is no birth and death of it. As in the poem with the crow and rabbit, representing sun and moon. Existing in the same space at the same time.

The 'Horned Rabbit' being the symbol for Non-existence. Thus if it does not exist, then how is it that it remains? Is it because it is the real suchness and the ultimate reality. Bhutatathata (chen-ru) mere - consciousness. This is the mystery of non-existence. What is 'it' that remains?

Jack Kerouac, "Beginingless and Endless also means Presentmomentless! There is no eternity! No present moment! No NOW. Wheeeee!"

"Emptiness is not interested in emptiness....."
Nat Shazi

Afterwards:

The Thought of Nat Shazi
Paul Dolinsky, Editor; www.thegoldenlantern.com

Expanding our minds, Nat Shazi takes us on a fantastic journey through the realms of metaphysics, shamanism, and even ordinary experience, ending the book with an account of a sweat lodge ceremony at the Lakota tribe. The book also includes some original ancient Chinese stories including children's stories. A wonderful treat that drips goodness through the whole series of poems, like a luscious ice cream topping on a hot summer day, are the poet's paintings, almost all in color. There is a generous helping- approximately 15 paintings and 5 photos (the book is 178 pp).

The poems are very lyrical and evocative. They are like windows that allow us to get closer to the experiences described in the book. In non-dualism there is no creation, only the discriminating mind that distinguishes between mine and not mine, or any subject-object relation. Narrative poems include two literal and figurative journey poems, those of the peacock and the whale (in "Sky's Night"), towards the sun, in soaring language.

There is a basic sequence to the book. It moves from non-dualism and the metaphysical, to the realms of nature and human beings, and finally the shamanistic realms of transformation- the inner and outer levels of people-and as they affect others. Aspects of the poet's own work as brakeman on a train, and maintaining a furnace at the power plant are included.

Each poem is complete unto itself, but is also a gateway, between a past and a future moment of the every day, which is an opportunity to practice No-Mind, Non-Dualistic approach to experience.

Lets move through the text to convey a sense of how the poet tells his stories. For instance, fairly eary in the book, after several poems on non-dualism, we have the Lantern Poem in the Oregon cabin, "Sikan Taza' themeless Meditation" which includes the line

The 'One Lamp'.
which is yet
Limitless in the
Lighting of other lamps.
an Alter-Light.
Always burning.
Influence of
One disciple,
may be limitless
& inexhaustible.

The next two poems, the practice described is
'Wu-Nien';
"Presents of the
Action of
No-thought."
"No-Mind, never matter".

(Ed.'s note: Actually similar to David Hume, in Western philosophy, who looks to the senses as the source of knowledge, a school of thought called empiricism.)

Then the poet, undoubtedly with his own work experience in mind, imagines, several poems later, the Buddha cleaning up the sky, and keeping things orderly. In a similar way, he observes in the following poem, "Legend of the Yawning Buddha," that it is not Satori, but continued vigilance at keeping one's mind clear that is the key.

In the next poem, as he drives to work, the poet momentarily mistakes the business sign as the moon, hence the title, "Burger King Moon, Deception in the Night Sky." The sign seems like the moon which stimulates thoughts of alchemical transformation, the burning off of the dross of consciousness, which takes the poet right to his job of maintaining the boiler at the power plant.

Several poems along, is the Straw Lady of the garden poem. "She is a scarecrow whose photograph is shown." But in the poet's eye the scarecrow is also its own idealized form of the spirit of grace, "Grace". one of my favorites in its simplicity and beauty, with wonderful photographs. Then, in the following poem, "Returning Another Sea Shore," the poet returns to the sea shore as an old man. He doesn't know if he'll be remembered by the place itself. This is the ending: Sound of the ocean and waves the same.
Light, same.
Turning back,

my footprints in the sand.
Now I'm remembered, the
tide takes me back to sea.
Now a hawk in the sky,
recognizes me and
I am welcomed.

There is wit and pithiness too, as in "Desire and Attachment
Stolen." A Buddhist sense of lack of attachment is, in effect,
promoted by government which garnishes the poet's already
minimal wage.

Presented to you now
in a conscripted way.
No-choice left
but to give it up….
    ….
Being forced
To see-through
your attachments.
'Purse-string' view.
Desires having
become obvious,
stepping back.
The falling away
of desire.
An obliviousness
now presenting itself.
Time distancing

V e.

itself from an
attachment no
longer held.

   And another example of the poet's wit and insight is his
response to the spiritual guide discussing breaking through the
karma of past lives and choosing objects of desire to reflect
upon.

"Take an object you want."
Examples; bird's nest, representing
Love of Nature.
Monetary bonds, wealth.
Books, knowledge.
Watch, longevity & age.
I look, and I think.
"What if I want to
take my willingness?"
"Your will, done!"
 The story telling and poems from everyday experience show
that it is our discriminating mind that keeps us from seeing
things as they are, as non-duel in their natural state.
We just need to remain open to this possibility, perceiving
things with an open mind, rather than with a closed one, so to
speak.
   This insight spreads to the imagination as well. Writing as
Wang Shang Shazi, the poet writes about ghost and bi-
locations, and revenge among other things. The book ends
With a personal account of a Lakota sweat lodge ceremony.

Contents

V.

VII.

Paintings & Photographs

1. Horned Rabbit
2. Black Butterfly/silver tip
4. Sansuikyo: 'The Rivers & Mountains Walking Forever '
7. Mongolian Moon Robe
9. Cranes in Moon Light
11. Elephant Walk
14. Bluejay
25. Lamp Charm
29. Rain, Screened, Backporch
43. Laughing Buddha
47. Mount Adams
53. Lady Scarecrow
56. Garden Tool Shed
75. Owls
82. 'Horned Lady'
86. Self - Portrait
87. Self - Portrait / Point Ryes National Sea Shore
94. Whale in Clouds
100. 'Yangtong the Peacock'

1.

ASAT

Singing as dusk sets. Twilight over the desert,
Stars and blackness came.
Mystery of Non-existence,
A horned rabbit remained.

2

Sijo Poems

The Sky Never Moves

3

Sijo: Sansuikyo, "The Rivers and Mountain
Walking Forever"
A fluttering black butterfly,
  with silver edged wings.
Dances in the air, beguine.
  Hollow clearing in the woods.

Observation; the phenomena,
winged Zen, transparent.

In the nature of things,
  existing in the moment.
Dead-giveaway, it's now become.
  eye-catching, here & now.
Undisturbed: oscillate, dart, float.
  The sky, never moves.

Be as the mountains & rivers,
  They walk on forever,
Neither high nor low have width.

4

Yet can reach the farthest seashore.
To be as the mountains & just sit.
  Sitting Zazen, serene.

Sansuikyo : Rivers & Mountains Walking Forever

5

10,000 Mile Railroad Track

Ekayana - One Vehicle
(Non-consciousness)
Search for

Last one out, 10,000 Buddha's
City changed the door out!

Five yrs. old as Rory Calhoune
Callaway went, that -a -Way.

Mystery, Non - Existance
by Hsyan-tsang.
Mere-Consiousness.

Discovered one mo. before
publish date, search 20 years.

First card, received for purchase   rebate
coupon for free pie.

6

In a dream delivered from
west to east, oceans rain storm

Wei-Wu-Wei, action of non-action
Without thoughts, ashes gray.

Braided rope, Shinto Shrine
Sitting still. The secret way.

Journey Ended, Dharma Temple
Lakasana , found Asat.

Game Ended, Continuum, endlessly,
in my own den.

Quit chasing the sun from the sky;
sky set, moons gone, arriving home.

Year of the Dragon 2000
SansEra

Mongolian Death robe

Natures Pathways

"Save the Nioborara River".
          Nebraska, 'Flatwater'.
Populous environment, sand hill cranes,
                    migrating south.
"Cranes Meadow', Platte River.
Observation deck, viewing cranes.
High in the sky, the sun.

8

Alda café, sack lunch.
Binoculars, sun glinted off.
Hundreds & hundreds of cranes landing.
Whoop! Jumping, Wings Flapping.
Cellophaned chicken salad sand.
          Guidebook: Sand Hill Cranes.

Marshy sand bars, sun soaked.
Viewed, standing, one legged.

Neck bent down, wings back, pecking.
Bacteriophage, climbing leg.
Metaphor for sand hill cranes.
        Lost in native environment.

Cranes in Moonlight

10

'Sijo' Driftwood, wet soaked

Roaring tides, breaking on jutted rocks,
                    Splashes high.
Yet receding backwards, depressed swirling
                    pools left.
Cycles of the Moon, wet sand line.
          Sandpiper hopping, wet feet.

Eddies running around, driftwood. Lying
                    motionless, still.
Hand sand scoop & bucket. Wet filled
                    sand, overturned.
Sea Shell ! edge sticking out. Hand held
          prize for digging, wet with sand.

Sea-Gulls flying, air drifting. Current
                    washing ashore.

Prolonging times ending, Stretching beyond
the horizons.
Footprints in the sand, this morning.
Moons tide, leaving not a trace.

Pratyeka Buddha

The private man, alone, to himself.
Living Pratyeka Buddha.
No body's business, but his.

Thinking his own private thoughts.
Answers to no one, cept self.
Understands all, and gestalts it.

Hearing only WunGong.
Knowing that it is his calling,
He responds in his own druthers.
In harmony & balance.
Existing not in accordance with others,
Individual walking about.

Going where & when he wants;
As per, in existence, just self.
To others, unconcerned,
Mind me not, as I'm not you.

Heeding not to others.
Pratyeka Buddha, like an elephant.

Poems were inspired from the 'Zen' newsletter, "Prairie Wind". A man in prison in the prison group ask the Roshi. When surrounded by evil and darkness what action should I take? Usually if surrounded by 'Tigers', one should be a Tiger. But in your case, you don't want to be like them. Thus you should be an 'Elephant'. Walk like an Elephant keeping a positive and bright aura against evil and darkness.

Roof of the World

Skeletal remains of flowers & leaves.
The sky knows the age.
Hidden in a crevice on Mt. Everest.
Winded off by times passage.
Decaying leaves & twigs.
When was last falls winter?
Spring blooms in the gutter off of the roof.

The Ancients
Living Amongst Us

Gliding 500 miles,
Two thousand ft. in the sky,
Raising on the heat thermals,
Spiraling upwards to sail,
Are Kettles of Cranes.
12,000 Cranes per ½ mile in River,

9 million years old,
Standing 6" deep in water.
Platte river, ten thousand years,
These are the Ancients among us.
Humans in geological time,
Blink of an eye, one-fifty,

Outstretched wings, leaping,
High in the air, corn throwing,
Bowing ritual, mating dance,
Mating for 25 years.
Melting pot, the Platte River.
Singles bar for Sandhill Cranes.

Worked So Hard

Ten & ½ yrs. working in a Steel Plant,
Janitor.
Drinking beer every night, yearly.
After 4 the "Blues".
Forgetting the pain, Billy Holiday. The
mind has changed now.
Wouldn't give to the jobs thought,
Trying to steal consciousness.
Deterioration of thigh bone. Helped not
by Alcohol.
Completely unaware of this.
Bastardization of Walking

Twisted femur out of socket, on 'Free'
wood list, loading.
Insert 'Non-natural', left hip. VA.
waited, Seven months.
Insult to Injury, wood stolen. Empty,
barren grass stain.

17

Poems
Wandering Tribe, The Fagowe

Tribe, The 'Fagowe'
nomadic wandering tribe,
great plains, legend has told.
the tribe known as the 'Fagowe',
states, "Where the Fagowe".
never knowing whence,
we've come from, nor where we are going.

wondering around, not knowing
to where they are going.
A group of the blind leading,
one of the blind, who doesn't know.
the vast panorama unseen.
Hands on shoulders following.

roving in search of the dwelling,
the habitat, not known.
one of the blind leading the group,
the following of the blind.
unobservable, lost!
fagowe tribe, "where the f _ _ k are we?"

Brakeman
'Dharma Bum'
14 Stanzas

Grip, Lantern
strapped to handle.
BN - Rear Brakeman,
on work train.
Auburn, NE. sandpits.

Riding in the Gondola
on the way-car, Caboose.
12 hr. night job.
evening sun setting,
Nebraska plain twilight.

Movement in the culvert
amongst the brush.
An Indian standing up.
Looked back, quickly.
Could have sworn,
I saw an Indian.

Return to my Automatic,

A 2"x 3"x1&½" piece of wood,
Stained & polished.
Lighter, swiveling bowl
& shotgun shell
contained within.

Fill the shotgun shell
with marijuana.
Turn over, rotate bowl.
Turn back & strike lighter.
holds about 3 hits.
Made by the
Handicapped, Retarded.
Lincoln, NE. subsidized
'Work Effort'.
I know I seen an Indian!
coming up from
Nebraska's red earth
Ghost of a Soul,
Long forgotten,
Remembered now.

Engineer calls on phone.
conductor says,

20

"3 miles to 'Break-Point'."

Got to 'Double' the hill.
as they call it.
Pays twice, for doubling.
that's an extra $100 bucks.
Stepping off on the move.
Walkie-Talkie
Tell Engineer to stop
& back up.
Manifest list in hand.
Car numbered, invoiced.
Know where to break the train.

"Three cars, - one car,
Stop."
Close angle-cocks
between cars.
Break the air hose
connection.
"go ahead".

Engineer takes front of train
up to siding.
Front brakeman

throws switch to enter.

Walk down right-of-way.
into trees for a wiz.

Full moon night
easy to see.
"So it all comes to this."
Quote by Jack Kerouac
on taking a wiz,
from 'Dharma Bums'.

Motors lights in sight,
returning.
Couple up rear of train.
Signal, Go - Ahead
with lantern.
Hop onto Flat - Car.

Leaning back
against the high bulkhead.

Stars, Moon & Motion
Hit on my Automatic

a couple times.

Jack 'Broke' for the
SanteFe
for a two yrs.
Now I'm one of his
People.
A Dharma Bum.

Fireflies Lighting

dusk, the arrival of darkness.
                    shadow taking over.
but wait, just there, a spark of light!
                    lingering for a moment.
lighting bugs, awakened now.
                    dance of light. on - off - on

observed through porch window.
enow a spark ! lights darkness,
luminous yellow movement.
            flashing on & fleeting, then off.

trailing the flash, hand caught,

some grass & fireflies held in glass jar,

a lantern for the porch.
The night now becomes you, in light.
an eternal proposal,
your girls finger now has light.
pasted yellow luminous light shinning,
                loves return, smiles bright.

Dhyana Poetry

Poem for the 'Diamond Sutra'

Time, Time
How can it be
Some not knowing
Thinking ; coming & going.

Know that it be
Illusions lust

24

Thrust ……

Breaking through
Barriers of time.
What was there
To unwind ?

Just our minds
Now knowing

Joyous wanderers
We be
Floating in Cosmic Sea

Through all
times eternity.

   Kakusei

'Sikan Taza'
Themeless Meditation

Lamp Charm

26

The source of
All themes.

Self-Discovery,
Not taught.
Although it is
by the Tibetans.

Thus providing
Witness of the
Validity.
Authenticated.
Confirming that I
Must have meditated before.
Or reaching a
Higher Threshold
Am being taught
by a higher
Consciousness'.
Taught 'Lamp Meditation'
in the Oregon cabin.
The 'One Lamp'.
which is yet
Limitless in the

Lighting of other lamps,

an Alter -Light.
Always burning.
Influence of
One disciple,
may be limitless
& inexhaustible.
Mirrored reflections
are limitless.

How to capture
the Lamp.
Then to take it.
Or yourself to a
Higher Plane.

There your Lamp is
Many & Different
Colors & Shapes
Transfinite, Unlimited,

Boundless & Infinite.

Now sitting &

Meditating
with your Lamp,
in Sikan Taza.
Having a thought
on Something.
The Aspect of
'Jnana'.
Wisdom in your
Meditation,
Comes to be!
Since it is the
Source of All Themes.
It will be presented,
In a couple days.

Ekayana found!
One Vehicle,
Non-Consciousness'.
"Asat," the Mystery
Of Non-Existence.
The "Samdhinirmocana Mahayana Sutra."

'BHUTATATHATA' (chen-ru)
Zen Master

Absolute
in transmigatory
form.

          Opposing
          Nirvana.

Asat,

the mystery,   Non-Existence.
Ancients & Buddha's'

          SansEra; All

Ageless. timeless,
dateless, infinite.

        No epoch,
        Everlasting.

And to this

        Ancient Traveler
You've come   Wandering
"Seeking the
Way,   Tao."
His reply,   "Legato!'
Having no   interruption
Continuous, endless, eternal.

"Walk on
Pass the   Twelfth of Never.
The day,   After that!"

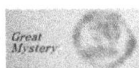

Great
Mystery

'Not Anyone to Nobody'

Zazen Meditation
By quieting the mind
& quelling thoughts,
One becomes
Tranquil & Serene.
Monkey leaping,
Branch to branch
Has been subjugated.
Following no
Thoughts any longer,
Mind has become
Pacific Sea,
Calm, vast & open.
Sky, clear & blue.
No waves of thoughts
 To disrupt it.
Internal dialogue,
Stopped!
Ego has no place

to cling to or be.
Quiescent of the

Mind, now mellowed
Out & relaxed.
State of 'MO'
Having been
Achieved.
NO one - Nothing.
Serene, Contemplation,
All that remains.

Practicing the meditations
of the 'Sandhimoricana Sutra,
'The Mystery of
Non-Existence.'
"ASAT"
Concentrating the mind.
Focusing on the
'Dhyana'.
No one or Anybody
Remains.

What; has been

Vanquished,
Begs the question,
'What'?
Awoken enow.
'Wu -Nien';
"Presents of the
Action of
No-thought."
"No-mind, never matter,
No matter , never mind
Non-mind, 'Wu-hsin'.

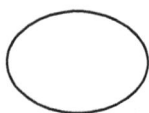

Eat this,
& have a
Cup of Tea.

Ethereal Meditation

An open view.
Jacuzzi in front,
through window.
Sitting high up
on stone steps,
in steam booth.

Steam rising.
Meditation in
the ethereal space.
Vaporous, as the
steam fills the room.

Sitting in
Ether Space.
No air in
Astral World.
Concentration
on Space
being you,

instead of you
being Space.
Breathing is Easy.

'Dharmalaksana'

Perceiving a Phantasm,
spirit or a Dead person?
Transmigration of Soul.
Signs, verification ~ self.
To change, amend, Past Life's Karma.
Oneself recognized!

Trans ~ state, Past Life Incarnation,
Fathom the clear meaning.

A bequeathal from Samsara,
Butalathata forms.
In the present, oppose Nirvana.
Seeing through bad Karma,

Viewed in Akastic record room.
Quandary presented.
Realization of mistakes.

Giving up Past for Present.
Clear and present danger.
Comprehended, the Ghost of the Past!

Soul
SansEra

'Sun Faced Buddha,
Moon Faced Buddha'

Dragon Sun Robe
Black crow on
Red Sun Disk.
Life

Dragon Moon Robe
Rabbit on
White Moon Disk.
Death

Full moon of October.
Moon light
at 2 a.m.
Sun light
at 2 p.m.
Only difference,

heat & humidity.

Color of Autumn.
Changing,
Falling leaves.
Death in a
Blanket of colors.

4 Seasons,
Evolving into Spring.
Life Everlasting.
Symbol,
White Leaf.

Crow on branch
Above.
Rabbit on ground
Below.

Life & Death
Symbols.
Co-existing in
the same space.

Universal Janitor

Before Sakyamuni
there was
Tahoe'.
& still waiting
in the wings.
Mitafu (Matiera),
the coming Buddha.

Can you imagine
the Supreme Buddha,
Out there, somewhere
among the galaxy of stars.
With a Whisk Broom
& Dust pan.

Sweeping up
Cosmic Debris
from exploding stars
in the galaxy.
Not leaving a trace.

All neat & tidy
for the Advent of
the next Buddha.

Dawning of the
'Age of Aquarius',
is upon us now.
Just wait for it.
What's one click,
one mile, one sec., an
hour, a milli-sec., an
epoch, a eon,
day, year, a century &
millennium
in Cosmic Quanta
of time?

The Universal Janitor
say's,
"Meet yaw round the
corner. In an half an hour."

P.S. Callaway - he went
"That - a - way"
                    Kakusei,

            Another World,
            Another Age

' Legend of the Yawning Buddha'

"Laugh, I thought I'd die."
The Kensho, Satori experience.
An awakening, enlightenment!
A sudden unlocking
of the minds pre-settings.
Releasing one from the
bondage he'd been held in.

A break-through, an insight
Into Sunyata the void.
In which all 'things'
are possible.
Usually has the expression
of laughter.

A release of hitherto
blocked passages
into the 'True & Real'.

Your preconceived mental
concepts, and interpretations
Shattered - all at once!
Your understanding,
having been derived from
particular instances or
occurrences.
No longer can support
your mental Structure.
The Roman Pantheon
laid to waste & ruin.

This release of your bonds
frees one from their
mental constraints.
Thoughts, emotions, senses
Are all opened now to the
'True & Real Natural'
state of mind.

A new panorama, eyes unveiled.

Those pent-up restrictions,
self imposed, released.
Uncontrolled laughter.
The expression of your Gestalts.

This enjoyment shared with
your colleagues, fellow monks.
Yet, now you are caught
in your satori.
Bringing a 'Yawn' from
the master.

You do not yet know, Continuance!
The eternal vigilances that
one Must sustain
In order to grow and
mature in the 'New Realm'.
    WungGong

ASAT   Mystery of Non-Existence

Burger King Moon
'Deception in the Night Sky'

For two nights,
looked for
full moon.
Then, on the third,
there it was
directly in my path

driving towards work.

As I got closer
printing started
to appear inside
the disk.
Then a hamburger.
Burger King Moon.

Laughing, looked over to
2 a.m. in the night sky.
A yellow crescent wisp
hung in the night.
The moon just coming
out of darkness.

The calendar I'd
been looking at
had it wrong.
It's in it's beginning phase.
A celestial root, called
Mind of Tao.

'The Crescent Moon Furnace'
This furnace is
the light of the mind,
Tao shining.

"Jade flowers grow,
in the cinnabar crucible,
mercury is level.
Blending harmoniously by
power of fire,
seeds have yellow sprouts,
which gradually
grow and develop."

Burning away
a person's mundane ness.
Mind of Tao
is represented
as a furnace.
Where this light shines,
All falsehood vanishes.

One becomes a sage
and an immortal.
Entering my job mind
the 'Coal-fired Boiler'
at the Power Plant.   SansEra
               Great Mystery

'Empyreal Mountain'

Mount Adams

Seeming to rest on the clouds
The 'Empyreal Mountain'
Raising into the either.
Majestic in its lofty elevation.
An ocean of clouds at the shore.
Sky above, Sky below.
An underlying substratum foundation.
The Roman Pantheon crumbles,
"And the walls came down. All the way to
Hell. Never saw them when they were
standing, never saw them when they fell."
Towering above on an Ocean of Clouds.
A formidable presence, the 'Empyreal
Mountain'.

Mt. Adams   Washington State,
                        Elva. 12,276 ft.
                            Long. 46`12'
08.68" N.
                        Lat. 121`29'
27.22 W.

rain sounds, thunder rolls
birds, chirp & whistle
the cat lies
in the screened window sill
a Scotch Mist hangs outside

' Spira Miralibis'

Couch Shell
Contains within it
A Spira Miralibis.
Revealing the Matrix
of the most perfect
Symmetrical form
in the Universe.

'Helix' Trajectory
Multiple turns
Converging to a
Focal point;
The focus,

Distinctness
of an Image.

Polar equation
r = ab <u>bo</u>

Matrix: Determinant
Mathematical objects.
a Vector,
Zero or more
Dimensional objects.
Two dimensional
Number arrays.

Logarithmic spiral
Adhering to the same
Mathematic laws.
Each enfolding
Whorl.
Describes the
Line of life.

This graphic
Representation
Presenting:
A Wave,
Right Triangle.
Protractor,
Two perfect circles,
 French Curve,
Line of Volume
& Force, &
Pi, 3.14

With a Rectangle
Window from the
Center of the Vortex
Expanding right.
When viewed into.
Presenting a
Different, Dimension.

All axis's
can merge &

Spin-off to a
Different focus
Point.

This line
Mirrored at once.
In patterns of
Nature &
Process of
Evolution itself.

Straw lady of the Garden

Evoking a presence
that at once captures the sight,
Expanding it over the entire garden.
tomatoes, cucumbers, melons, corn, peppers
the vines.
Are all vibrant with enriched colors & hues.
This lady, slight & lank,
moves through the garden with
the Sun's Light!
Her costume like a
multi-colored flower,
Blouse & long skirt,
her straw hat , wide brimmed.
A tall figure, her arms
gracefully extend as
they reach out.
Slender hands & fingers.
Her movement a delight.
Her gardening.

It's obvious in it's
glistening reception.
That this gardens
in love with her.
Though only a Scarecrow,
made of straw,
She has the heart
of enrichment.
A lovelier garden has never existed.
Garden tool shed's
her home.
With the tools, fertilizers, pied pots & seeds.
Her name ?
Grace.

Returning, Another Sea Shore

when I arrive
will I still be remembered ?
do you think that I'll be recognized ?
aged, hair turned white,
will it remember the years
or be all new?

does it anticipate my return,

as I draw near.

57

will I be welcomed or just viewed looking ?

oceans the same
sky same, clouds have changed.
waves crash in, recede out again, same.
sand feels deeper,
same at ocean tide, wet.
sound of ocean and waves the same.
light, same.
turning back,
my footprints in the sand.
now I'm remembered, the
tide takes me back to sea.
now a hawk in the sky,
recognizes me and
I am welcomed.

Akastic Record

Cloaked in hooded
white robe.
Unseen to others
in the Bardol
of Past Lives.

Passing through
Life after Life.
In search of
experiences, causes,
attachments.
which karmic ally
affect this present life.

Lead by my guide,
a Puma Shaman Lady.
Instructed to;

feelingly – see , the vision.
From the file cabinet drawer.
A cassette tape
placed into the pocket
of the shroud.
Your Akastic Record.

59

Since your 'First'
Inception.
Every thought, emotion,
attachment, deed
as has been preserved
in light.
Manifesting as your
Karma for
Future Lives.

In viewing these
scenes.
Your karma's

attachment is presented.
Your present life's
predicament revealed.
Now able to discern,
Why? the causes for.
To remedy, heal or
change this karma.
That controls your
present life.
Releasing you from
the binds, so as
to advance.

Now led to another room.

60

In this room,
Dusty with cobwebs.
a window, fireplace mantle.
Table with books & papers
strewed about.

On the mantel, objects.
Guide says,
"Take an object you want."
Examples; bird's nest, representing
Love of Nature.
Monetary Bonds, wealth.
Books, knowledge.
Watch, longevity & age.
I look, and think.
"What if I want to take
'My willingness?'"
"Your Will, done!"

Another World,

Another Age

61

Mine or Yours

Whose people do you belong to?
The ones who buy the Pork loin in the Supermarket and
then cut it for a sandwich?
Those who exchange individual socks in the drawer
cause there's a hole in one heel?
Or do they climb a six foot step-ladder to fill their bird-
feeder, are they bird-people.
Ring - "March of Dimes", calling. I'm sure they're not
your people.
But then again, maybe the Letter-Carrier is. Do you
think?
I know you're not a T.V. commercial people or do you
buy the 'Hot Pockets', ham or pizza?
Do you shovel the snow for your elderly neighbor. Are
you one of his people?
Or are you the one, "I don't give a damn.", when your
spouse complains?
Are you the one who ignores the radio singer telling
you who you are?

Or do you behave and let him be you.
"Look at me!" speaks the Television set. Are you them,
or do you continue on to the kitchen?
Do you step back when you should step forward, or
vise versa.
Are you in the Dance, Or not!
Are you hard to get along with? Or do
you live in repose with your people?

Awakening: Dreaming

I dreamed; that I was awake,
Eating toast, drinking milk,
Walking about, talking aloud.
Upon awakening,
I ate toast, drank milk,
Walked about and talked aloud,
Dreaming that
I'd already eaten toast, drunk milk.
Walked about and talked aloud.
I awoke, found myself standing in
The middle of a dream.
Dreaming that I'd awakened.

'Antidotal Healing Remedies,

take the medicine'

In a search for knowledge.
& to rid ourselves of Afflictions & Attachments.
            'Zen Mind, Beginners Mind',
Suzuki Roshi, - -
        There's no excuse for not sitting.
                'No Shin',
D.T. Suzuki - -
At the 'heart' of the problem
the Buddha spoke,
                'Lotus Sutra',
'Juana', knowledge,
                Vajra thunderbolt.
'Diamond Sutra', expounded by
Gautama Siddhartha.
& Gary Snyder say
                'Tribe together',
As kindred spirits in , 'Turtle Island',
Pulitzer prize for words.
Action of Non-action,
                'Wei Wu Wei'

states; these pieces are unsaid, never written.

'Posthumous Pieces'
'Treasury of the Eye', Dogen's
Investigative, dissertations,
                    ' Shobogenzo',
on what's, what.
Sri Arobindo's , Encyclopedia
White covers, Gold lettering,
                    ' A to Z ',
enough ! close the door.
Transmigration of the Soul,
Tibetan Book of the Dead,
                    'Bardo Thedol'
Reward for finding,
            'Samdhinirmocana Mahayana Sutra' .
searched for, for 20 yrs.
1st. new credit card purchase
   (Coupon for 'Free Pie!)
Esoteric Mind Control,
                'Mikkyo Hand Mudras'
by Ninja Grand Master.
The Eight Consciousnesses,
            in '30 Verses on
Mere- Consciousness'.
Swati Ganguly, Yogacara Yoga,
                    65
mind & body.

'Namu Amita Budsu',

repetitive Mantra.
Guarantees rebirth in the 'Pure Land of
Amitba Buddha'.
This comprehensive, all incursive list.
brought to conclusion in
'Death & Fame'.
Accentuated by Alan Ginsberg,
Last poems of a Dying Man.
'Clear Blue Sky'.

Krishnamurti
'Master of Dialogue'
"Let me ask you, This?"

Direct confrontation
Is where he's at.
Tete - a - tete
Leading questions & answers.

Billed as the 'Next Messiah'.
Theosophical Society taught him.
He saw through the scam,
Realized he couldn't fulfill Destiny.

Fill back on his upbringing.
Teaching, training, presentation.

Facial expressions, mannerisms, elocutions.
An extremely high level of dialogue.

Leading the questioner to the next question
2.
Investigating, argumentation and resolve.
Which, he's already answered.
As in a 'Chess Game', four to seven
                                    moves ahead.
Becoming Krishnamurti, 'World Renowned
                                    Master'.
'Messiah of the 21st. Century'.

When if you look ahead of the lead.
And query him back, leading behind.
Going to - . Again and then again, again.
You've got him! He's caught.

He stumbles on his words and answers.
Already pre-conceived.
Trying to re-enter the original hypothesis.
Yet he can't!

Understanding, advised in 'thought',
Watch the Baseball or Football.
3.

Or, <u>Be where your at.</u>
"Play - Ball."
Man on third, man on 1st.
One out, you're behind two runs.
Bottom of the Eight.
Many! Plenty of variables.

"What should we do?"

'Desire & Attachment, Stolen'

The thief of your
desire & attachments
sequestered by
the Government.
Conscription of
Disability Insurance
Called - Up !

isolating your needs
to what you can afford.
Your Minimum Wage.

Attachments garnished.
Pilfering your wage.
Extinguishing all
superficial needs.
Wiping out their attachment.

Years of Meditation.
Sitting Zazen,
Buddhist Philosophy
of losing
Desire & attachment.
Presented to you now
in a Conscripted way.
No-choice left
but to give it up.
Inconsequential,
negligible & unimportant.
Your attachments to desires !

Being forced

to see-through
your attachments.
'Purse-string', view.
Desires having

become obvious,
stepping back.
The falling away
of desire.
An obliviousness
now presenting itself.
Time distancing
itself from an
attachment no
longer held.

Can one really
put any blame on
Social Security Disability.
Dropping attachment
to desire not totally
Gestated by Zazen.
Now quenched
& wiped out.

By the 'Flies',
in your wallet.

{ Gata, Gata, ParaGata,

ParasomGata,
Budhi Sava}

Gone, Gone, Gone Beyond,
To that Place,
Hail the Goer !

'Nickel Fortune Cookies'
Luncheon Special

Golden Dragon Palace
guard dog statues
at entrance
winding stone path
approach
natural native
grasses
arched bridge
Pond

Large goldfish
& black catfish
golden dragon
on door

Handed menu
by host
seated underneath
large Chinese
Landscape painting
Waitress placing
Tea pot down
Black Oolong tea
She catches
My eye
What a fox!
Ready,
To order?
Come back
'Nickel Fortune Cookie'
Lunch special
2 fried Wontons

Egg Drop soup
Tso's pork
Steamed rice
$5.95
We'll have the

72

5 cent lunch
Tea cups & pot
Similar
To mine
'Chang Tao Lin'
Chinese character
Fierce warrior
Protecting a man's
Soul
From specters
Rita, our waitress
Serves up lunch
She's really
Friendly
Allowing opportunity
To parley &
Taking injections

Of thought
Laughing, smiling
Witty reply
This nickel lunch
Really tastes
Good
Got Rita's
Thoughts
In my mouth
Enjoying the tea

73

watching Rita
Across room
By windows
She doesn't walk
'Flows like a
Rushing brook'
Do I dare
Hit on her?

Fortune cookies
are set on table

We'll there be
anything else?
Come back

"Opportunity is
watching you"
says fortune cookie

Looking to where
Rita's at
She's watching me
signal her over
let's see if she's
as sweet as
the fortune cookies

74

Yes, what can
I get you?
Besides the check
your address

where I'll
pick you up
tomorrow night
at 7 pm.

Smiling brightly
& stepping back
she motions to
herself
stepping two steps
forward
bending to my ear
It's the Yellow house
from the corner
12th & E
behind Quick Shop

Golden Dragon
door
Opened for us
leaving
Up over bridge

Pond below

Sky clear blue
Lucky
'Nickel Fortune Cookie'

'Yet, There I Remain'

Between twilight
& dark,
What is there?
Shadow.
Does the shadow
leave at darkness?

Natural world,
needs light for
Shadow.
Darkness

doesn't see
Shadow.

76

Darkness doesn't
know light.
Light has never

seen darkness,
only Shadow.
Where did
I go,
darkness doesn't
see me.

Fireflies light
the Night.
No darkness,
or light.
Only a shadow
remains.

As the light,
dims away.
Gone

77

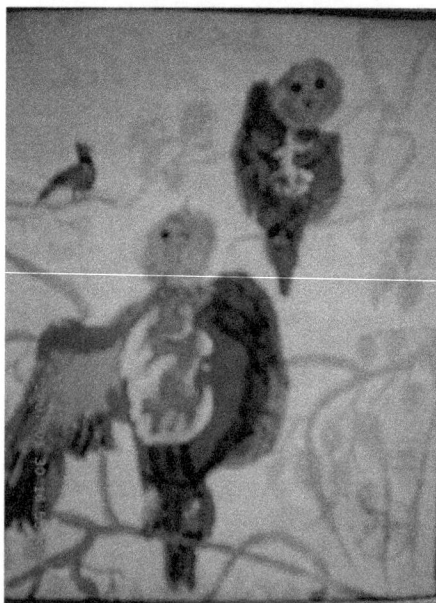

Wisdom: Is Silently Seen

sitting silently in the morning,
they watch,
as I do.

morning coffee before sunrise.
on the back porch.
seen through screened windows.

78

owls watching.

they must be watching me.
attention caught them,
as I sat.

two owls; bobbing their heads,
sideways, up & down.
cigarette smoking,
coffee drinking.

looking; they've moved,
silently flying,
to a higher branch.

must be their radar.
not even a flap in the breeze.
two young off-spring,
having joined them.

now the wood pile ash,
sitting atop.
diet consist of potassium.

sunlight shines off leaves.
return, through broken window.
my garage, barn owls, roosting.

just as the sun setting,
lengthens its shadow.

they've returned,

to the same light shading.
only the knowledge of sight sees them.
silently watching.

praja-parmitti sutra.
dhyana wisdom.
sitting twice a day,
morning & evening.
rising of thought-consciousness'.

turn of your head & then back.
And they're gone, no fan-fare.
a firefly blinks at me.
darkness presenting itself.

Song of Life

-" Hi Niswa 'Vita ' Ki Ni"-
(we shall live again)

Spirit brothers of the past
Look around you
See how it last ....

Everything changing, yet we remaining

The first shall be the last
& the last shall be the first

We have arrived again
From where, we know not when

Here and now we be
Look around, can you see
It is the way it will always be
This is life eternally.............
 —"hi niswa 'vita' ki ni"

Rocks, trees, birds & bees
Sky flow, mind flow
What do we really know

Except that this here be the flow..........

Just lay back, let go

Float on, & on & on
This here rainbow sprays
A never ending rainbow day

Here & now we be
Look around, can you see

It is the way it will always be
This is ...., Life's eternity.........
–"hi niswa 'vita' ki ni"–

Here we find ourselves once more
Moving through different doors
Seeking that special La'moor
Open this door..............
* –"hi niswa 'vita' ki ni"–*

Rainbows are both beginnings & ends
Open your heart, let one shine in
Begin .... Begin...........
Take it to its rightful end

Star light, star birth
Welcome back here on earth

If this be the end

82

Then surly you've already been

Here & now we be
Look around, can you see
It is the way it will always be
This is life's mystery
 -"hi niswa 'vita' ki ni"-

"Golden Triangle"

Dyana meditation on
'Praja Parmiti Sutra'

meditating wisdom
Buddha's & Ancients
passing along
their insight.

Gaining intuition
of knowledge.
seat–of–the–pants
intellectual capacity.
Sixth sense.
Conceptionalized
Immediately,
Yet the inconceivable.

Apparent,
Is not.
Appearance of it
Beyond your
Knowledge.
From the 'Golden Triangle'
Geometry book.

"And yet, still
There shall be,
Veil after Veil."

Dark Secret
Black Space, nothing but moon,
Orange, full and here.
Engulfed, nothing left. Darkness
And there I remain.

Epitaph
This alone, move on.
Not empty, strength of sight.
Snow, open and white.
Silent message of friendship
There's no room at the inn.

Kakusei

Remembering a future life,

Mustn't fall asleep.
The light of the day,
Like a pressed flower between the pages.

Flying Fish

Sunlight off ocean waves.
Eyes glint at the reflection.
Deep and hollow, on the rim waves break.
A symphony, maestro directed.
Then just there, a brilliant flash,
A flying fish out of the blue.

Another World, Another Age

From times previous, next times future.
 Dream deep, profound.

Wave of sea to deliver,
Another Seashore-
Centuries journey, Pass on.

View in the lamp of dark.

Another World, another Age

Unrung
WunGong Calling

The summons
from the bell,
ringing.
"For Whom the
Bell Tolls."
It definitely
Tolls for Thee,
without doubt.
If you
Hear WunGong !

Can't you Hear
the Calling ?
WunGong.
the initiate
Whisper,
in your Mind.
Before the
Bell is Rung.

Clearly Seen !
the Unrung,

WunGong.
Summons
Whispering,
  GONG!

Heiku's

Mental whisper,
initiated.
WunGong calling.

No sound.
Yet I See it Ringing.
WunGong!

Your calling.
Without doubt!
Hearing WunGong.

Clearly Seen !
The Un-Rung, Gong.

Signature Poem

SansEra

Sans Era Until The End
Sky Set, Moons Gone
Pass The Faded Night
Shifting Sands Of The Ages
The Skyline Sees Beyond

Nat Shazi – Self Portrait – SansEra

Self Portrait

Point Ryes National Sea Shore

Cliff at 'McClure's Beach
'Point Ryes National Sea Shore'

Ocean eddies
in pools
around rocks,   Golden Starfish
recedes,   Sea Shells
splash in again.   Waves
                                      Foot prints
                                      in sand

my, boots
hung around neck.

                                            High Cliff

confronts me.
Really high   Climb it.
do I dare?   Climb it!
     Point Ryes, telling me to?
Boots on
Study cliff,   Were to begin.

Look to

were I'm going.
of cliff

Climbing up
Look down,
Go back down

Cliffs face

Crevices
small hand holds.
Look up,
ahead,
for path.

now.
Lost my foot

out-bound.
Body

against cliff.

Best navigation
face.

1/3 of the way
think about it.
not to late.

Sandy, quartz
graphite.

Search

½ way up
Slipped.
hold.
Aware of posture,

flat now

Slipped again.

trying to find
foot hold.
going to fall.
even more scared
Heart beating fast,
I'd be killed
or severely injured.

Scared, afraid
Look down
now.
too High.

Wait for it.
relax, flat on rock.
Look up
a hand hold
Remember!
Keenness of

Calm down
don't move!
Search for it.

No foot step
Awareness.
See it,
Look farther up

for another.
Have to look

down.
find different
foot step.

so as to

reach
Did it,
moving cautiously,

Relax again,

Looking up again

In the cliff

Sort of a

I'll be
just make it
to the

sitting in
Eating

Next hand hold.

Alright!

Breathe,
Let it be.

See it,
Crop-out.

An Ice-plant
red-flowered.
hollow.

alright

hollow.
¾ of way
hollow crop-out.
Ice-plant

95

& flower.

View is
fantastic.
Looking out

rest of the way
just a little
up ravine,
upward,

to the top.
Make like a
on all fours.

Walking along
upright.
Beach & Ocean

Wind in face,

Over Pacific Ocean.
Check it out,
up.
more climbing.
crevassed

Gentle, slanting
rise,

Mountain Goat,

Up the slope.

Top of Cliff.

Far below.
Sky Scene.

Children's Stories

At eventide an insects lorn
a black whales lullaby
Chimes a chorus of soundings
from the constellations
Give into the night

Sky's Night

Tungyai 屯该

By, Nat Shazi

Listen very closely now. There are two bright

Stars in the constellations Lyra and Aquila.

Between them at 2 a.m. above the heavens swims

a Great Whale.

Now this very whale, one bright night, began to

swim above the

moon. She was very happy and her song was

coming from her

heart. Her celestial song, dancing off of the light

reflected from the

moon on the clouds, changed in its frequency.

When it changed, her celestial song's vibration

turned to one note. That note reached beyond her

consciousness. Somewhere

out there at 2 a.m. in the night's Sky, a sea star

floating on the waves of eternity, received her

song.   In her celestial oceans a light glimmered.

High above her out of

her left eye was a sea star. The whale turned

heading for that star. In her mind, a cerebral song

to sing a reply to her heart's song. Thrill-

ing her and sending a quiver down her spine,

which penetrated

through to her soul and in her heart, that glimmer

blazed out into the heavens.

It changed the resonant shrill of her song.

Harmonizing it into an

enchanting melody. Chimes as a chorus of

soundings told her to dive deep. Into the sky she

dove, beyond her depth. A great sea route opened

and the chorus changed to a lullaby. The chimes

now

revealed as a trident and a soft sandy voice spoke,

" Let go to the

night and all children shall dream in you."

As she began to fall asleep the vastness of the

sea opened onto

the splendor of the sky's night. In her ecstasy she

began to dream

and all the stars in the constellations heard the

lullaby.

At eventide swimming above

A black whales lullaby

Chimes a chorus of soundings

From the constellations

Give into the night

Ancient Chinese Story

Destiny's Romance

by Sikan Tao Shen

One day heaven told of Yangtong, the peacock. There in the clouds under the pearly haze of the mountain range of Kong Jian in 'Open Valley' in the midst of the mountain peaks of Jin Quo and Bao shi Nuan lu lies, Clear Lake. Where the story was told of how Yangtong became one of the immortals. The great mystery now to be revealed.

Living in the province of Yao Parg. One shrouded mist filled day in the bamboo grove,

Yangtong came upon a split bamboo, and
a hollow feeling enveloping him. He was
lonely.

Staying concealed in the grove all these

years, Maturing his practice, he had become

quite accomplished, and was now a mirror

unto himself. What had been revealed by the

split bamboo was that he'd finished. Without

further examination, he knew that it was time

to leave the confines of the bamboo grove.

The loneliness that Yangtong felt was that he
had no one to share his life with, nor anyone
who cared, His light having been kept unseen.
Coming out in a clearing near a tall pine, the

mountains beckoned him. He must leave Yao
Parg. Eating wild raspberries, meandering into
the forest but strayed near

105

the edge. A quiet came over him, as dusk
settled in. The berries having refreshed his
body, he now began to eat the nuts lying on
the pine needles. A coolness to the air caught
his attention. A lake glistened in front of him
as the magenta of the sky announced sunset.
The light of the symmetry in the mountains
clouds enticed him to take flight.
   The glowing gold splendor of the sunset
aligned him into the winds eye. As he glided
to a landing at the lakes edge, a brilliancy of
white struck him, reflected from a high
prominence. After getting a drink he meditated
on this point of reflection. There in the lake,
was the moon, casting up a silvery gloss off
the water, his
figure visible in a luminous light.
   Yangtong felt the tenderness of a presence.

He began to feel the attraction of a lover and wondered where she could be. Looking skyward, the movement of the clouds brought

his mind to the dark silkiness of the waves. The winds movement over the lake echoed his thoughts back to him. This caused the waves to drift to their own times movement.

Taking flight, raising to the skyline, landing in a pine tree, Yangtong folded his wings.

A soft breeze came up just then gently whispering his comb caressing, 'come up'. As he began to dream, he remembered, listen to the night, he fell asleep.

The blackness of the night engulfed the resonance of the stars. It presented a clear perception, unlike any other night. The silence lent to an audibility of sight. The night awakened, clearly seen. The blackness of the night engulfed the resonance of the stars.

The answer having been seen, his thoughts became feeling. His dispassion dropped.

Raising his head he saw that his loneliness
didn't exist ! He knew now that the emptiness
he'd been carrying around, had

turned into a loneliness which left him feeling
unwelcome, in his own self.

He knew now, the compassion evident. In the
darkness of the night, the dragon had revealed
the great mystery silently.

Yangtong awoke before the darkness of the
night had retreated. He liked this time before
daybreak when the shadows of the night were
caught by morning. The night awakening now,
the lights attention here and there, Yangtong
stirred in his roast, nights darkness hiding
away.

A light breeze came up. Seeing through the
branches the tenor of the pine needles fighting
the breeze, waking his senses. The pine
needles wavered through his comb catching
the breeze. He looked out through the
branches at the mountains, the light of the day
already up. Opening his wings and shaking off

the dew, Yangtong pushed off.

His wings catch the colors intensity, his

strength stand out from the pines. The direction of his wings carry him up. Looking at the line of his ascent, seeing through the sky, there was an airy flower of white cut ice.

The sight of the crystal light was being so splendid, that it makes last evenings charm present. He remembered the silvery gloss the moon had cast from the lake, the tenderness of a presence. The breeze that had came up. He realized he'd seen her ! At a glance in the gentleness that was a whisper.

He looked up at the point of reflection he'd meditated on last night. The light in his wings lifted him. Taking the flight he moved in the direction of the wind. In his mind he now knew. The juices peaches his what he wanted and had an eye for. Those
peaches existed in Kong Jian in Open Valley.

During one of his rests he glanced up at the sun. The light that shown through his eyes

illuminated his vision.

Seeing through the sky, his eyes were unveiled. The clear light visible, its forms aspects seen, life's presence discovered. The presence of existence revealed. The scenery's panorama
tacitly shown. Life was beyond himself. Yet this existence gave it presence.

Passing through destiny's passage, Liberation ! An open space. Completely at ease the invisible barrier lifted. The scene having shifted. The way always present.

A single thought unborn, light showers silently throughout eternity. Turning his head quickly, the sky gave flight to his wings, and the sun light carried him out into the infinite. The light of his soul being was burnt from an earthy existence to an eternal light, changing

the color of his fan tails eyes to a higher
vibration.

110

The day was brilliant, the illuminant luster on
the leaves and blossoms, and the reflection off
the lake. Lifting the eyes was the whiteness of
the clouds. The mountains
had an edge to them that presented a sharpness
to the colors. The flower's colors held a
fadeless harmony of light. The sky was so
clear that the radiance of the day presented the
most picturesque sight.
   He looked to the breeze over the leaves of
the peach tree. The leaves catch the light,
a glowing gold standing in relief to the sky.
   The totality of being emulated from beyond
the real world . The sky are peaches.
   Alighting in a peach tree his fan fully
opened, in his eyes he could see the light
showering every which way.
   In the open air beyond his fans sweep the
light of the day having seen her.
   The aged split bamboo bids you.

Kakusei

111

Death Warrant
By Meng Zheng ren

It had taken me half the evening to make

my way up the mountain. The steps that I'd

taken being measured and true.

The crystal clearness off the frozen branches

standing in relief to the brightness that

reflected off the deep snow from the full

moon. The appearance of my ghost of

fourteen years ago being chilled from

without, as my foot steps

hardened almost instantly. The openness of

the space leaving the ghost of the past in the

hardened impressions of my footprints as I

passed. Moving through the cold still open air

I saw the Kaide Tavern.

   It had been several years now since my
disappearance. The plum wine tasting fresh,
it's warmth relaxing. The air in the tavern
making an impression of welcome, the chair
which I was seated in holding the heat in a
solid form. Inviting was the fire in the large
hearth. The atmosphere in the tavern an open
reception from the weather outside, as the
snow melted from my boots leaving a puddle.
Having been in the tavern now a little over
half an hour.
Seated at my table, the daily newspaper, bottle
of wine, candle and cup stand to keep my

wine warm. Remembering the ice white of the cold full moon. As my breath emitted the smoke, there in the smoke I saw their thoughts in their glare through my mind. Raising up independently was the cigarette smoke as I raised my cup to my lips. there in front of me I saw him. Glancing up to my left and turning

My chin out after finishing my drink I diverted his attention to the death warrant hanging on the pillar behind me. His stately proud smiling eyes started in surprise, a sense of shock masking his face. Having taken his sense of pleasure from him. Turning the right side of my head behind him and looking right, the imposter was seen. Leaning against the wall drinking a mug of beer.

He'd been so happy a moment before, the master mind of the conspiracy; standing tall in his uniform coat, fat belly hanging out, pickled egg in one hand, his small ivory pipe

in the other. Now confused as to why there
was a death warrant for his friend for the
death of Wang Shang Shazi.

The atmosphere in the bar suddenly
changed as the gramophone reechoed the
song, "The Wanderer" carrying the air.

This time catching unawares the two at the
end of the bar. Glancing up to where the music
came from, a tall haughty figure with a high
top knot, long silvery beard in long brown
slicker coat poured his wine into his glass.

Time was now on my side, having caught
them all unawares and starting them out of
their presence of their mind.
Suddenly brought back into their memory, the
remembrance of fourteen years ago. My
disappearance, the subsequent impersonation,
this present encounter; bringing back their
memories, to me, Wang Shang Shazi.

They worm their way into your mind and eat the substance that sustains thought. Controlling the conversation so as to set your mind's events in theirs. Lying to your face with every thought and every spoken word they say. Deadening your thoughts so you can't hear your own minds echo. The

impersonation beginning there.

Should you speak your own mind or talk back to them they become dumb, dull and lifeless. Being mad at first and then changing the conversation and as they do, in your moment of blankness, stealing your presence of mind. After which their benumbed mind presents itself. Leaving your mind blank looking at theirs. Forcing you to be who they are! Should you not, and be your own soul they retaliate by punishing you.

Bouncing, dancing, orange white, changing colors of light. The fire from the hearth's roaring flames bringing memories past, present.

Pouring coffee, reading the newspaper, rolling cigarettes, listening to the radio. Hearing thinking, seeing thinking, you woke up. Within the veil of night, the weaving of the screen that is dreaming, was seen through.

Seeing who the dreaming was. Foxes red revealed, hidden in the fabric of the dream, the apparition's unclean shadow shaded off. Legend has it that the disincarnate spirits of red foxes like to steal and impersonate a man's mind.

Dreaming yourself into the future as Zarcoff, you escaped! Zarcoff being your own invention. An extravagant character, so abnormal that his maverick ways of thought confused their mental capacity completely. Walking in different character, appearing in different guises, speaking in different dialects. You'd been able to present yourself in their dream without them recognizing you. You left them in a frenzy, chasing their tails in confusion.

And there in the future, you began to plan your comeback and revenge. Going into their very psychic, turning the tables on them.

116

Screening them, appearing and disappearing, out foxing the fox. Placing a cankerworm in their minds. Using your wit and cunning, with your uncanny ability to out maneuver them, and then, with your own lamp meditation, in your sleep you stole their mind from them. They didn't know what to do. and you laughed, bringing about their total ruin.

Witching time now approaching. The masquerade about to be exposed, you poured some more wine and set it on the cup stand over the candle to keep it warm and laughed. The sbag players in high merriment, ringing in the ears, the cling- cling as they threw their coins in. The gayety of the rooms light sending a pleasurable feeling through the tavern. Reflecting the orange yellow light from the fire the beer glasses caught my eyes. The waiter hurrying to the sbag room with another tray of draft.

117

Looking over at the smoke raising up where Huan Xing was standing near the gramophone, I noticed my cohort's tail was showing. Dreaming in the future I'd stayed at a Taoist monastery where the silver fox, Huan Xing Ming, an awakened dream, and I had become close friends.

Possessing magical powers and benevolent spirits he taught me how to unweave the dream fabric. Spending all my sleep time within Huan Xing's consciousness he had taught me the art of unconscious dreaming. Which led to the exposure of the red foxes. Now here in the dream the two of us awake and ready to unleash our plan and the subsequent disrobing of the animals.

Caught between their mental screen I had actually disappeared. Hidden away in their fox hole. Their deceit masquerading in the play as

my life. This carouse having a smell of vinegar about it.

Snapping out of my reflection, the memory of the vinegar setting my mind back to the scenario of the plan about to unfold. Glancing over at the warden seated at the bar, then, back at the foxes at the end of the bar, I saw that the scene was now set. The killers of Wang Shang Shazi's mind about to be arrested.

Disguised as Zarcoff they hadn't suspected a thing when I walked into the tavern, Being two places at once when I actually wasn't anywhere at all, according to the accounts of my disappearance.

Seeing streaming forth from Huan Xing's wine bottle the purple plum wine, that had a life! Seeing the awakened dream, now it was time!

The silver fox raised his left eye in the direction of the end of the bar. Appearing

before my eyes a spirit reached out and set a big garlic on the bar in front of the specter who'd been imprisoning me. He reeked, turning and putting his hand on the shoulder of the other.

Looking up behind the bar in shock the four of them saw you in the mirror. The spirit of Wang Shang Shazi. Seated at your table in front of the death warrant.

Paralyzed in their shock; hands off, divested of robes, ears, noses and tails showing.

The warden rose shackling the four of them and dragging them out past the death warrant. Were he hung them from the pines outside the window.

In the dreams vision Wang shang stood up sans Zarcoff and walked over to the bar, Huan Xing welcoming him.

SansEra

Death Document

德阿　斗門

韓佛日大　　佛日

裏	貴	啊
呢	色阿	磁體怎
的阿	裏	佩斯哦
斗門	佛日	擦普

| からけてちめとくいめかとにら | 色阿 | 熱はせさ |
| | 滿 | 和 |

佩斯哦

Mongolian Dragon Robe

Sand Under

In Light

Summer Sky

By; He Zaiwai Shidai

(Sans Era)

Extending to the horizon vast and high the suns light.
Open over the plains, lasting and timeless. Set atop my pony.
With my basket of peonies and poppies still are the flowers.
As the pony's mane laces across them.

The sand under Powder's hoofs brings my attention to him . Leaving the road instinctly, he knew the way. In my memory the happiness of the day

I'd received Powder.

123

Grandmother had summoned me in a most curious way.

First mentioning the fable about the dragon who'd torn his

Wings on a high mountain peck and then that I was to be

Present. Because the ancient writings, that the Mongolian

Lama had found revealed a secret, and that secret concerned

Me. I hadn't thought of the dragon fable in years and

Couldn't figure why she'd reminded me of it or what the

Secret could be. Somehow the two were connected and my

Curiosity was excited.

124

Powder too, was all charged with the strength of the

Excitement. When I'd tied the basket of flowers around his

Saddle horn he turned quickly, eyeing first me and then the

Flowers. Then as I mounted and sat he'd raised his head and

Whinnied.

Seeing the village ahead I pulled back on the reins

Softly but with some elasticity going through the rains.

This allowed Powder to slow down gradually to a walk. Pass-

ing in among the yurts we'd been noticed and the word had

125

spread cause just before I rounded the chiefs yurt my friend

Styr-tou- hua came running alone side.

Styr tou hua, dismounting and running around the front of

Power, Stone Flower embraced me.

"Have you come to see me ? Why has Powder his best saddle

on ?"

"Come along, Grandmother has summoned me. My mother told me

that it was a special visit. That's why Powder's best saddle

and the flowers. There for Grandmother.

As we approached Grandmother's yurt Dianzho (ignite)

and Yishing (all one's Life) came up to greet me.

They

wanted to play but has I had not yet seen grandma
our play–

ing would have to wait. Grand mother had been
standing in front of her yurt

watching. She had her arms folded and a very
pleasing smile.

"Hi Grandmother !"

"I thought this morning would never reach the
sky and

you'd arrive." Opening her arms and giving me a
big hug.

"Your outfit is so handsome."

As she started to take me inside I remembered
the

flowers. "Wait, I've brought you something." I

127

untied the

basket of flowers hurriedly and gave them to her.

"These are very pretty, thank you . Now com,
I've much

to tell you." And she led me inside.

After seating me on a rectangular pillow
grandma handed

me a raspberry drink mixed with some goats milk.
"There, that

should be refreshing after your ride. What has your
mother

told you about the ancient scroll the Lama found ?"

asked

grandmother.

"Only that it was found in a storage box with something

else and this would be special for me." I replied.

Grandmother smiled knowingly. "What does it mean?" I ask

spilling a little of the drink on my vest.

"Next month, June is your fifteenth birthday, is it not

Heng quo he?" Grandma said as she placed a pillow down in

front of me and sat down.

"Yes," I answered.

"Do you remember the ancient tale of the dragon?" asked grandmother.

"Sure, how he'd torn his wings on a high mountain

peck and couldn't get them repaired. So he went fishing and

got a another dragons wings, I remember."

129

"That's right, answered grandma, but the moral of the

story is the answer. How a dragon yawned and almost drowned.

Does this understand you?"

"Not really grandma, but what does this have to do with

the scroll?" I asked.

Grandmother smiled and then laughed as she got up

saying, "You would like some giaokeli cookies wouldn't you?"

"Grandmother,! What is it? You only make chocolate

cookies foe special events."

"Just be patient," answered grandmother on her way to

her kitchen space. Returning with the cookies and

handing me

a few. she said, "I ground some pistils from some Lantanas

flowers to give the giaokeli an orange flavor. And before I

forget, there are some cherry jelly roll-ups for your

friends and you. Now where was I?"

   "The dragon yawned and,"

   "O-yes," grandmother interrupted," well you see it's

like this. The dragon was asleep dreaming under the lake.

When the dragon with the torn wings paused to drink his

strawberry shake the dragon sleeping yawned,
giving himself

away. So the white dragon went with his suitcase
that he had

his wings in wearing his shoes to the lake with his
fishing

pole. When he caught the blue dragons wings he
almost drown.

Do you see now?"

"I understand now," Heng quohe said.

"Do you like the orange with the chocolate?"

grandmother asked.

"O yes," I replied.

"Thanks, I thought that would make them extra good. Now

here's where the story gets interesting. I'm going to fix

some coffee while we continue. Would you like some more

raspberry drink?" asked grandmother.

"Alright"

Grandmother said as she was mixing her goats milk and

coffee to a foamy froth, " The white dragon put his new

wings on and flew away. Having regained his true life.

Leaving his suitcase and shoes representing the false life

behind."

"Which brings us to the ancient scroll. This is such a

lucky karmic event for you, and all of us. I was stunned

when the Mongol Lama brought the storage box and showed me

the contents."

"Where is it Grandma?" I exclaimed surprised!

"It's right there, pointing to my left, you may bring

it over. Set it between us." answered Grandmother. "Our

clan, Ca'ng was named thus for our ability to blend with

the sands mind in the air rendering us hidden. Which is what

you've been all this time and we've been dreaming you. We

named you 'Across the River' cause your mind and place has

has always been beyond us and not where we were at. Meaning

that beyond our space something else was seeing you, always

drawing your attention there."

"To where? Grandmother." Quietly as in private, "Why am

I seeing beyond you?"

Grandmother quietly began to tell the story. "The Lama had

deciphered the ancient scroll and learned that we are

descendants of a Mongolian Prince and Princess of the third

rank. They were the Mongols of a former reign, before Ghengis

Khan's time. These Mongols had hidden away the princes

daughter. This would be your great-grandmother."

"Does this mean your mother?"

135

"Yes dear, and they hide her just before the warring

party destroyed their village. She would have been fourteen.

Her name was Lang de Sichou, which means 'Wave of Silk', but

she'd then become lost and a gypsy family had taken her in."

"Here is the important part Heng quo he. Lang de sichou

was about to be presented her Dragon Robe as a coming of age on her fifteenth birthday to womanhood. The robe had then

been put away into this storage box awaiting it's discovery.

"Do you begin to see who 'where' is that has always

seen where you are?" asked grandmother.

"I don't think I understand completely." I answered.

" Its your Great-Grandmother watching you." grandmother

said. "and the "where', is here in the storage box."

Grandmother looked at the box and then back at me.

"Open it, that's where your true life is and your destiny."

As I leaned forward to open the storage box grandmother

said. "This was 79 years ago. In the scroll the story is

told and the gypsy clan identified as our tribe and you

dear are the heir to this, your dragon robe."

137

As I took the dragon robe out of its keeping and began

to unfold it carefully grandmother said.

"Hold it up in front of you."

I did and grandmothers eyes and face smiled 'Aglow',

as tears began to run down her cheeks.

"Now I can see you Heng quo He. The C'ang will be

able to see into the light. Lets go outside.

"Yes, that's what I thought. The sky brings it all

out, here." Grandmother reached out for the robe, "Step

back farther."

"Oh!, grandmother in the light it's the summer sky."

The End

Mongolian Dragon Robe
Description

Vast character-auspicious, wishes for longevity

Axe-fir, sacrificial weapon, power to punish & behead

Fire symbol- thin, licking flames

Sun Disc- Red and contains a Raven

Fu symbol- Paired, school of discrimination, prototype

of Ying-Yang Symbol, dualistic forces of good and evil

Dragon- King of animals, Mongolian: 3 clawed- side face,

 third rank or below

Endless Knot

Mountains- Center of the universe, world mountain

Conch Shell- Sea monster (sh'en) changes form, see its

 characteristics image-bearing vapor rising out

 of giant conch shells

Dragon breath & Pavilion– 3 dimensional, supported on

mist or vapor, mirage (City of Sh'en)

Gourd– transmigration of soul

Jade– Ocean

Butterfly symbol– Longevity & happiness
140

Peony flower– Summer flowers of riches & honor. It conveys

hopes for greater advancement

Peach symbol– Long life, shown alone in combination with

happiness symbol

Cranes–'White birds', which dwelt on P;ing–lai

Shan, 'the

home of the Immortals', longevity

Bone– Protects ones head

White Leaf– Death; everlasting happiness
WunGong

Ancient Chinese Folktale
"Chinese Knotted
Tale"

'How the Siamese cat got the crook & bend or knot

in his tail.'

Long ago in a Buddhist Temple in the country of
Thailand. Then know as 'Siam'.
Lived a cat name of 'Dadara'. He was a silver point
Siamese cat. There are three categories: the silver point,
chocolate point and lilac point. Named such by their ear
markings.
Dadara was the temple cat. Having complete run of the
place. He liked to hang out in the kitchen. Where the
monks were preparing meals. Hoping to get them to
throw him some small fish pieces. Going out side then
to the Tool Shed looking for mice. Walking along atop
of the stone walled fences he was very audacious, bold
faced and brazen about his way.
The Abbot of the Temple, 'Lucky Star', some called it
the Monastery of the Red Star. His name "Sudden
Exposure", Given to him when his Master passed the

'Mantel' on to him. Because of his 'Abrupt' way of
giving 'realization/
awareness'. His spontaneity, an easy breezy way of
doing things.
"Sudden Exposure" liked to sit in the lecture hall for his
morning zazen meditation. The hall had large open
windows above the beams underneath the roof
overhang. Allowing the light of the morning to

experience the weather. The floor of the hall was polished dark teak wood with throw rugs near the raised podium.

Sitting each morning at 6 am. At around 6:23 am Dadara, the temple cat would 'come-to'. Experiencing his morning 'burn-outs', flights of fancy. Running and tearing around inside the temple willy-nilly. Dadara was a tall cat. By tall I mean that he had long legs and a thin sleek body. Gray, black and silver colored fur, short haired.

Every morning he would come running, tearing into the great hall in his 'burn-outs'. Running & sliding on the polished floor. Leaping onto the throw rugs causing them to slide. Then rolling and kneading with his claws before springing off and careening away. Right in front of the Master. Disrupting & disturbing his morning zazen. 'Sudden Exposure' having had enough of this

mischief.

When Dadara came running into the hall the next morning the Master was waiting for him. 'Sudden Exposure' reached behind himself picking up his whisk and throwing it at the floor in front of where Dadara's long legs were running too.

The whisk hit the floor bouncing up to Dadara's ankles, knocking him down. Flying sideways onto the floor and sliding to the carpet. Rolling over then Dadara lurched up right into the Master's waiting arms.

"Now I've got you, you ornery cat. I'll show you." and with an abrupt, spontaneous move. Grabbed Dadara's tail
with one hand. The other at the end whipping it around and through. Tying a knot in his tail. Holding Dadara up under his front legs now to face him. "There, you naughty cat, that will teach you not to create mischief during my zazen." Then throwing him onto the carpet, saying,

"Scat, now !"

Dadara turning over in mid-air, landing on his feet turned to the Master. Who looked him right in the forehead. Dadara bowed, his long legs bending. Sprang up & back running out of the great hall. With a new character and disposition. Now he had acquired that

144

'Haughty Air' that gives the Siamese cat his aloofness'. Looking down his nose at the 'rift-raft'.

Next morning at 6:23am. Dadara came running in. This time straight for the Master seated in his zazen posture on the podium. Stopping before him, his head bending forward, dropping a dead mouse on the carpet.

'Sudden Exposure', raised an eyebrow!

By SansEra

145

Shamanistic Stories

"Lakota Sweat Lodge"
Rosebud Indian Reservation
South Dakota

"Ahwho!",

the firm confirmation
the pipe is passed
sweet grass
spiraling smoke essences
lies on stone rocks
Flap thrown open
more hot rocks
passed in.

Flap closed
darkness
heat like a sauna
trapped inside
canvas sweat lodge
nostrils smell of sweet grass

146

lips tingle, hot

Yuwepi Man sings
Chant is repeated
by the eight of us
"Takashewa!"
Great Grandfather

speaking in Lakota language
Yuwepi man prays

"Ahwho!"
chanting
passing of pipe again
kakicka plant tobacco
heat stinging
unbearable
flap thrown open
air & light rush in

Can see everyone now
Yuwepi man
sits across from me
Alfred on my left

`147

ceremony for him
& two others
apprentice shamans
'Joe Running', Yuwepi Man
lights more sweet grass
reaches up pulls
flap down

darkness
"Takashewa"
chanting in unison

Pipe is passed to me
"Make a prayer."
"Takashewa,
Great Spirit
I Shazi pray
Alfred's recovery"
pass pipe to Alfred
"Ahwho!"
chanting
lips are hot
heat raising
others pray

148

as pipe is passed
in turn

In the darkness
you can see
eyes accustomed
everyone sweats

naked
it's crowded
Alfred has an
alcoholic problem
sweat lodge ceremony
to cure this
asking for spirit help
lips again burning
Light!
air & coolness
flap thrown open

"Ahwho!"
as the flap again is closed
high shrill
Chanting

149

following along
incredible high feeling
hitting on the pipe
passing it on

Flap opened
Yuwepi Man

exits
ceremony over
emerging
Full white moon
dark now
bond fire
to heat rocks
burning out
a dozen or so
Lakota tribe members
lounge on hillside
tend to fire
I'm handed a towel
told to get dressed

Real lightness

150

to body
totally Clear!
high consciousness'
feeling apparent
walking back now
talking with Alfred
& one of the young

apprentices
to the lodge
Ogallala Souix
Tribe

Many people
at least 3 dozen
young kids
old men
family's
women sitting up table
plates, bowls utensils
I'm seated at end
on far right
Alfred sits near center
with two apprentice

shamans

Minds- eye
sees a vision
an Elk with
large rack
Large iron crock-pot

passed among everyone
seated on floor
old in chairs
along back & side wall

It's Elk stew
as the lady
ladles me a bowl
cold tea to drink
flat, round Indian bread
bowl with fruit pieces
apple, orange, cantaloupe
grapes

Head of Sioux Lodge
makes statements

152

two apprentices now
Medicine Men
Alfred honored for
taking cure

Tied in a blanket

lying on floor, is
'Joe Running'
drum beating begins
kerosene lanterns
extinguished
Chanting
Minds-eye sees
medicine cords shaking
dancing above Yuwepi Man
along with
Eagle feather
Chanting & drumming
stopped
lanterns lit

'Joe running'

153

kneeling
dressed in
flannel shirt, jeans
moccasins &
red bandana
unbound - Magic
holding medicine cord

in one hand
& eagle feather in other
speaking in Lakota

Makes statement
"young boys
at track meet
will bring
happy news
congratulates
new shamans
& encourages Alfred
to continue
& use Spirit

Yuwepi Mans

154

demonstration
of Magic & foretelling
over
friendly atmosphere
and talking

In through the door

running
4 young bucks
to their parents
excited
They Won!
880 yds. relay at
Winner, SD.

by Nat Shazi

Spirit Catcher

Shaman Healing Ceremony

Laya, Shamanistic
Yuwepi
 Lone Wolf - Oregon West Coast
gift of coffee
& 'Wolf Mask'
rhythmic beating
drum, night darken
into shadow refection.

Full moon light
Summer Solstices.
Spaced 5 to 7 yds. apart,
Knee high grass.
Healing ceremony party
a trickling stream,
ridge high.
Tepee stacked wood.

Circle dancing around fire,
hands joined.

3 steps left, 1 back, Rt. over Lf.
1 step forward, Lf. over Rt.
3 steps Rt., 1 back, 1 step forward.
Repeat.

'Puma Indian Guide'
"get naked".
Army blanket covered.
Thrill down spine.
Eagle feather stroked.
"Announce yourself."

"Takashewa",
"Great Grandfather,
Sky & earth
from the fires center,
to the East, South, North, & West.
All sentient beings.
It is I,
Shazi"

Eagle feather
touching top of head.
Now I am shadow.
flickering reflections,
fire dances over everyone.
Night is black
As I now am.

Led by Guide, across circle.
West to East, to ridge.
deep pool
Laya across pool,
naked.
"Jump"
cold shock, entering water.
Arising
'Smack'!
egg-yolk on forehead.
Laya jumped too.

Towels & blankets,
Army wool warmth.
Circle rejoined.
"Tell Great Spirit,
why you've come."

"Takashewa, Great Spirit,
In all the Ten directions,
Winged ones, Earth bound,
Fishes of the sea, Creepy Crawlies.
In the light of this fire.
Shazi, ask for solace -
past lives bad karma.
present life, captive.
Release of bad karma."

Yuwepi guide Laya
hands over deer jaw bone,

Medicine pouch attached.

160

unearth when digging.
fire pit.

Scurrying noise,
shadow movement.
Direction -
my pack.
get dressed.

Healing ceremony
ended.
Lively, high-spirited
astir conversation.
Beat of drum,
leading out.
Progression back.
Route-step at fallen tree.
pairing up, talking now.

trailer house returned.

Guitar playing,
tea drinking.
Enjoyment
Anthropology Grad.
Thesis: Witness
totally blown away.

Gem stone,
swings over herb vials.
hand held
Stops over 'Wild Oats'.
A drop on the tongue
every morning.

Unpacking pack
Eagle feather
discovered.

Laya on phone.
"It's yours now,

162

Eagle feather
gift from,"
"Takashewa"

SansEra

www.ingramcontent.com/pod-product-compliance
Lightning Source LLC
Chambersburg PA
CBHW020515100426
42813CB00030B/3249/J